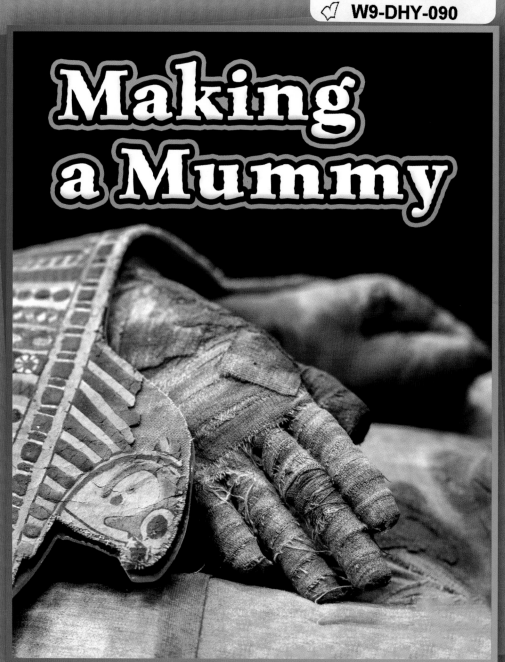

Making a Mummy

Dona Herweck Rice

Smithsonian

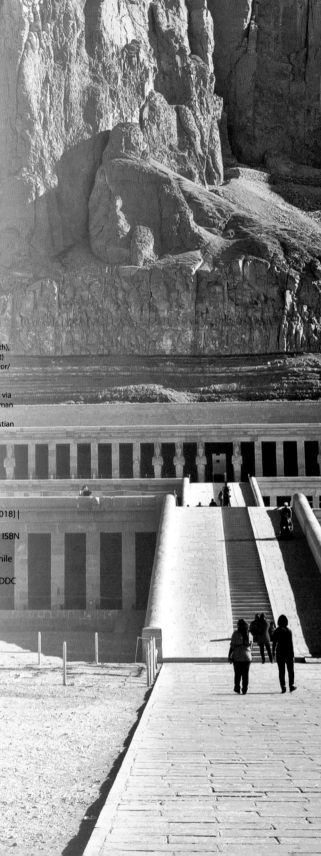

Contributing Author

Allison Duarte, M.A.

Consultants

Tamieka Grizzle, Ed.D.
K–5 STEM Lab Instructor
Harmony Leland Elementary School

Douglas H. Ubelaker
Curator and Senior Scientist
Smithsonian

Publishing Credits

Rachelle Cracchiolo, M.S.Ed., *Publisher*
Conni Medina, M.A.Ed., *Managing Editor*
Diana Kenney, M.A.Ed., NBCT, *Content Director*
Véronique Bos, *Creative Director*
June Kikuchi, *Content Director*
Robin Erickson, *Art Director*
Seth Rogers, *Editor*
Mindy Duits, *Senior Graphic Designer*
Smithsonian Science Education Center

Image Credits: back cover, pp.2–3, p.12 (both), p.16, p.22 (bottom), p.26 (both), p.27, p.28 © Smithsonian; p.4 (left) James Wibberding/Shutterstock; p.5 (right) Meunierd/Shutterstock; p.7 (right) Leemage/Bridgeman Images; p.8 J. R. Factor/Science Source; p.9 Andrea Izzotti/Shutterstock; p.10 Chronicle/Alamy; p.14 SSPL/Getty Images; p.15 (bottom) The Metropolitan Museum of Art, Rogers Fund and Edward S. Harkness Gift, 1920; p.17 (top) Stefano Bianchetti/Corbis via Getty Images; p.17 (bottom) De Agostini Picture Library/G. Dagli Orti/Bridgeman Images; p.18 (right) Interfoto/Alamy; p.19 (top) Bruno Ferrandez/AFP/Getty Images; p.20 Kenneth Garrett/National Geographic/Getty Images; p.23 Sebastian Kahnert/dpa/Alamy Live News; p.25 Carmen Jaspersen/dpa picture alliance/Alamy; all other images iStock and/or Shutterstock.

Library of Congress Cataloging-in-Publication Data

Names: Rice, Dona, author.
Title: Making a mummy / Dona Herweck Rice.
Description: Huntington Beach, CA : Teacher Created Materials, [2018] | Audience: K to grade 3. | Includes index.
Identifiers: LCCN 2017053172 (print) | LCCN 2017054061 (ebook) | ISBN 9781493869190 (e-book) | ISBN 9781493866793 (pbk.)
Subjects: LCSH: Mummies--Juvenile literature. | Embalming--Juvenile literature. | Egypt--Antiquities--Juvenile literature.
Classification: LCC GN293 (ebook) | LCC GN293 .R53 2018 (print) | DDC 393/.3--dc23
LC record available at https://lccn.loc.gov/2017053172

Smithsonian

Teacher Created Materials

5301 Oceanus Drive
Huntington Beach, CA 92649-1030
www.tcmpub.com

ISBN 978-1-4938-6679-3
© 2019 Teacher Created Materials, Inc.
Printed in China
Nordica.042018.CA21800320

Table of Contents

Speaking to the Dead

Buried beneath the city of Luxor lies the ancient city of Thebes. Both are in Egypt. One is the present, and one is the past. Luxor tells a story of modern life. But Thebes tells a story, too. The story is found in its **artifacts**. The people left behind also help tell the story.

Scientists today have found a piece of the story of Thebes below Luxor. There, they have unearthed mummies from tunnels and tombs. These are parts of a very old burial site. The mummies were so well **preserved** that the bodies look as though they are alive. Scientists know much more about mummies than they did long ago. A lot of the information comes straight from the mummies themselves. The truth is, the dead can tell a gripping story!

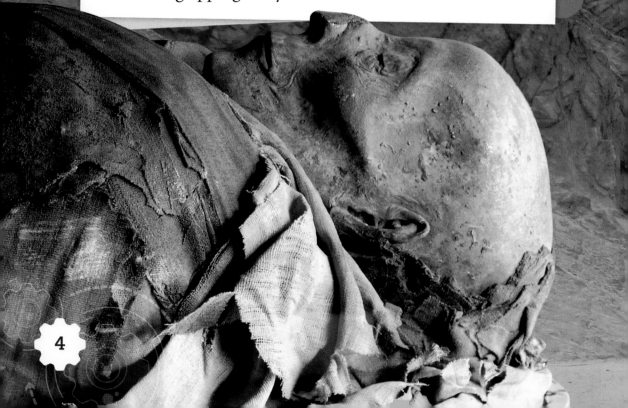

Men search for artifacts near Luxor.

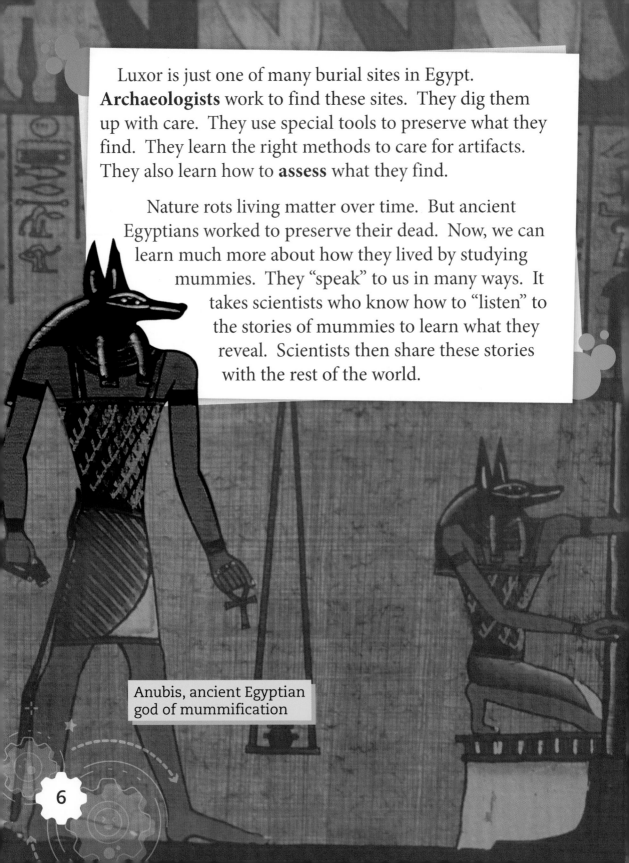

Luxor is just one of many burial sites in Egypt. **Archaeologists** work to find these sites. They dig them up with care. They use special tools to preserve what they find. They learn the right methods to care for artifacts. They also learn how to **assess** what they find.

Nature rots living matter over time. But ancient Egyptians worked to preserve their dead. Now, we can learn much more about how they lived by studying mummies. They "speak" to us in many ways. It takes scientists who know how to "listen" to the stories of mummies to learn what they reveal. Scientists then share these stories with the rest of the world.

Anubis, ancient Egyptian god of mummification

An archaeologist and his assistant examine an artifact.

Ancient Egyptians thought the soul needed its body after death. With its body, the soul had a chance at a better life after death.

Preserving the Body

Living things decay when they die. *Decay* means "to break down." The body is eaten by other living things. These include bacteria. Bacteria are tiny **organisms**. They are made of a single cell and are so small that they cannot be seen. But they exist all over the world in large numbers.

A mummy is a body that has been preserved. This means that things were done by people or in nature to keep the body whole. At first, Egyptians buried their dead in pits in the desert sand. This is known as a pit burial. The dry heat preserved the bodies. Bacteria do not live well there. So there is nothing to decay the body. It may shrink and darken, but it does not decay.

Egyptians saw what happened to the dead. They wondered whether there were other ways to get the same result.

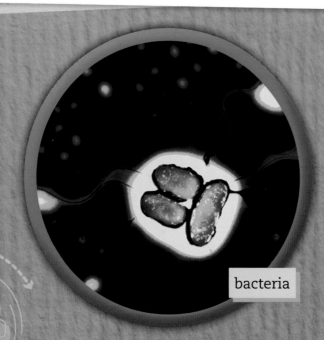

bacteria

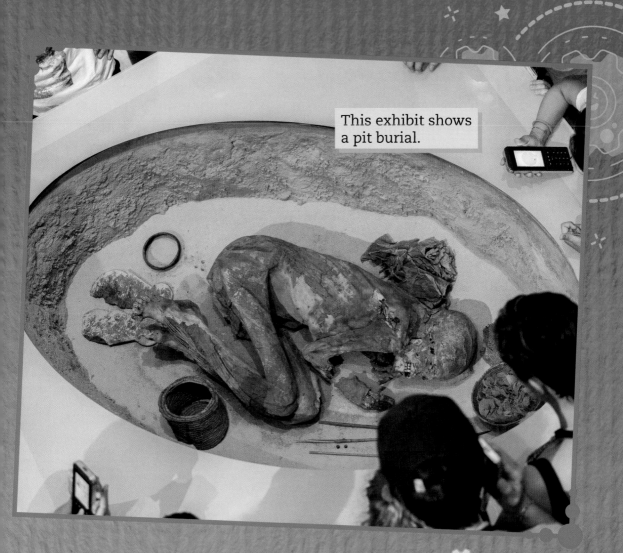

This exhibit shows a pit burial.

SCIENCE

Keeping Decay Away

The bacteria that decay bodies do not grow well in hot, dry areas or extremely cold, icy places. They do not grow well in swampy **bogs** either. Mosses that grow in these bogs keep bacteria away. Bacteria also need oxygen to survive. If a body is kept in an airtight place, it will not decay. Mummies have been found in each of these areas.

Trial and Error

One problem with a pit burial was that ancient Egyptians believed the spirit needed to sleep there. They did not like that idea because sand pits could easily be dug up and robbed. A better plan was needed.

Egyptians began to build coffins and tombs. They dug holes in the sand and lined them with stone. The dead were placed inside boxes and then the stone tomb. It would be hard for anyone to **desecrate** (DES-uh-crayt) such a burial place. But they still had to find a way to preserve the body.

The first known attempt at man-made mummies involved wrapping bodies. They were wrapped tightly in **linen** and placed in tombs. Egyptians thought this would protect the bodies the same way the dry sand did. It did not. The bodies did not stay intact.

A desecrated tomb is discovered.

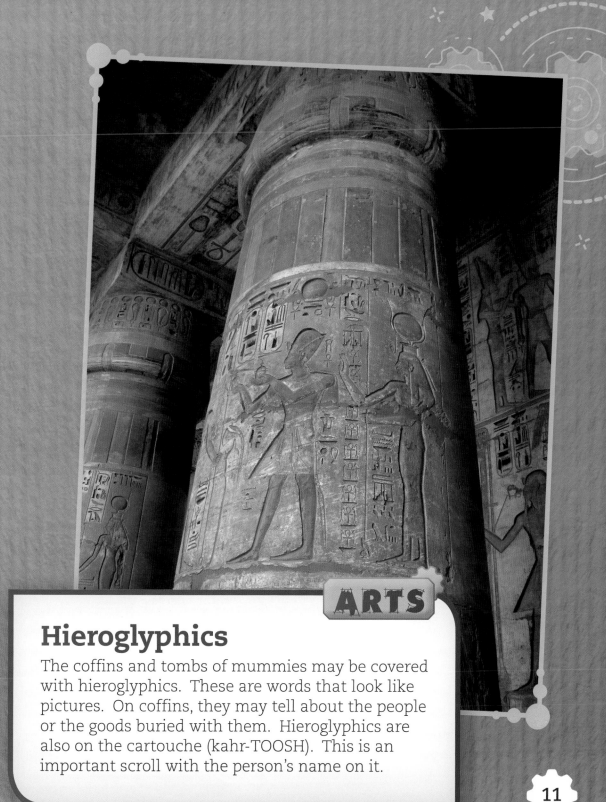

Hieroglyphics

The coffins and tombs of mummies may be covered with hieroglyphics. These are words that look like pictures. On coffins, they may tell about the people or the goods buried with them. Hieroglyphics are also on the cartouche (kahr-TOOSH). This is an important scroll with the person's name on it.

Next, Egyptians tried to preserve bodies by soaking the linens in resin. Resin is a plant-based substance. It can be used to preserve things. They had some success with this method. The skin was preserved. But the bodies still decayed. The innards rotted, and then the rot spread to other tissue. Egyptians learned that decay starts with a body's organs.

So, they tried taking out some organs before the bodies were wrapped. They preserved the organs with resin. Later, the organs were buried with the body. Next, linens were soaked in resin and stuffed in the body. This helped stop the decay and give the body shape. Cuts in the body were sealed with resin as well. Then, bodies were wrapped like they were before. This method worked better than any other had. But Egyptians kept working to improve the end result.

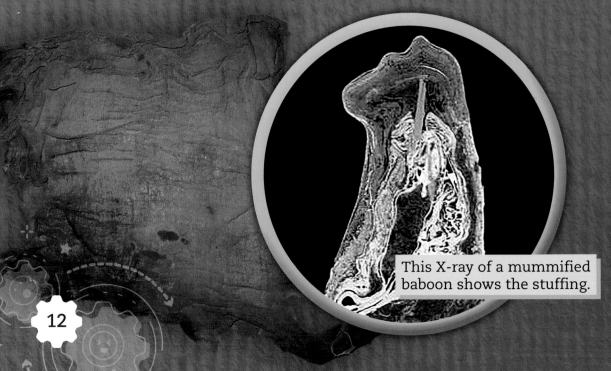

This X-ray of a mummified baboon shows the stuffing.

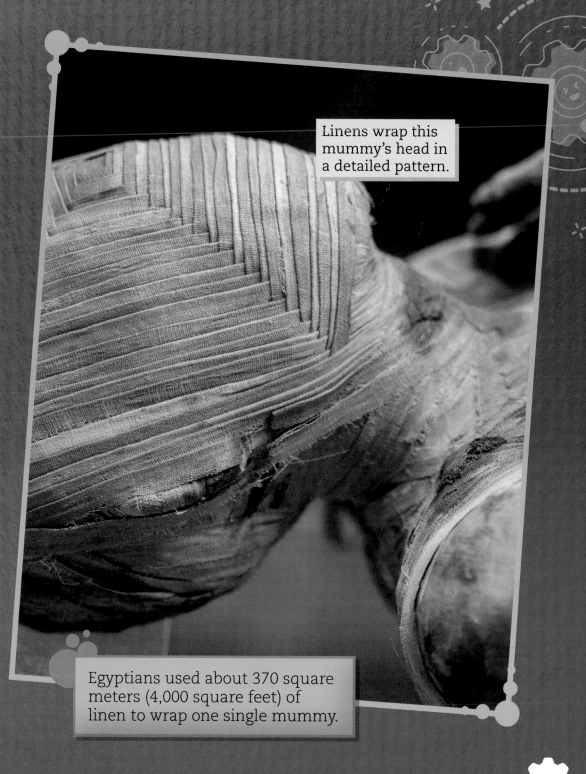

Linens wrap this mummy's head in a detailed pattern.

Egyptians used about 370 square meters (4,000 square feet) of linen to wrap one single mummy.

Success!

It took some time, but the Egyptians finally found a way to keep bacteria from the body. They did this through a process called **embalming**.

To begin, the body was washed. This ritual prepared it for the afterlife. Then, it was placed on a table to be **dissected** (dye-SEC-ted).

First, they removed the brain. The embalmers broke through a bone inside the nose. They shoved a hook into the brain to soften it. Then, they pulled out the brain through the nose. They rinsed the skull with water and added resin. (No one thought the brain was needed in the afterlife.)

The embalmers then cut a slit along the left side of the torso. They removed the liver, intestines, and stomach. They cut the chest and removed the lungs but left the heart. They believed the heart was too important to remove.

embalming hooks

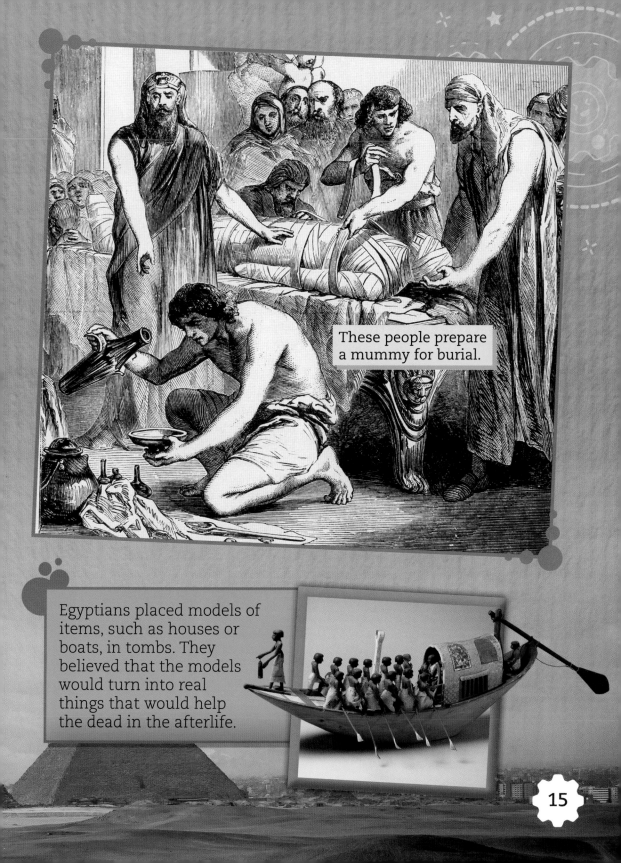

These people prepare a mummy for burial.

Egyptians placed models of items, such as houses or boats, in tombs. They believed that the models would turn into real things that would help the dead in the afterlife.

The organs were then cleaned, treated with resin, wrapped in linen, and placed in **canopic jars**. The jars were placed in the tomb. The chest was rinsed with wine, filled with spices, and stuffed with linens. Then, the body was filled and covered with a powder called **natron**. It was left to dry for 40 days.

natron

When it had dried, embalmers removed the stuffing. Then, they packed it with fresh natron and linens soaked in resin. They filled the body with sawdust and coated it with resin.

At last, it was time to wrap the body. This was a long, sacred process. Much linen was needed. The embalmers prayed and cast spells as they wrapped. **Amulets** were placed among the wraps for protection.

canopic jars

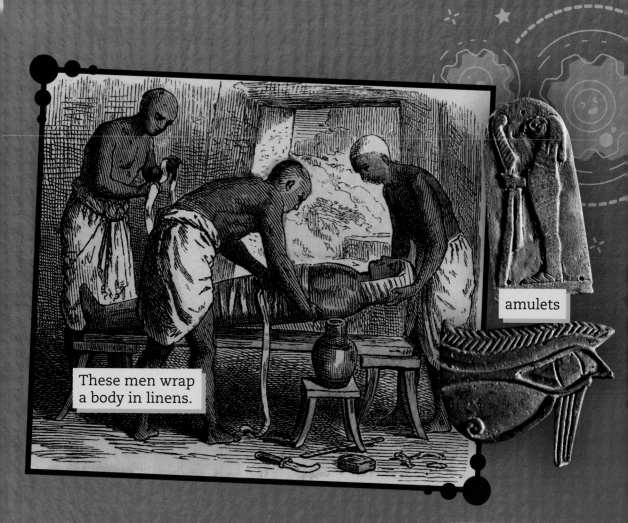

These men wrap a body in linens.

amulets

MATHEMATICS

Pyramids

After a body was wrapped, it was placed in a pyramid. The base of each pyramid is a perfect square. Each corner is a right angle. The builders used right triangles made of rope and wood as measuring tools. They placed a triangle at each corner to plot out the square base. Then, they used rope to measure each side and made them equal.

drawing of the Great Pyramid of Giza from above

Windows to the Past

Scientists have studied mummies for a long time. They study the science behind them. They want to know how and why mummies were made. So they study what people did to make them. They also study what happens in nature to create mummies. For example, a person might become trapped in a bog. Or he or she might be frozen and become buried in ice. Nature preserves the body over time.

But scientists also study more than just *what* happens. They study the culture of mummies. The culture is *why* mummies were made. It is also all the things people do to help the dead. They might make masks to help their souls find their bodies. Or they might bury mummies with goods they will need in the afterlife.

ancient Egyptian scroll

Egyptian mummy's mask

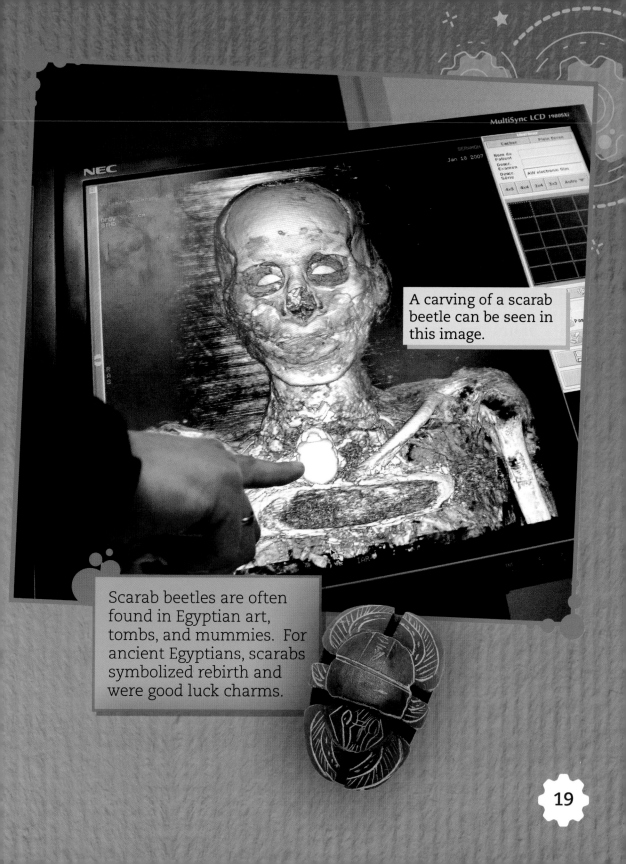

A carving of a scarab beetle can be seen in this image.

Scarab beetles are often found in Egyptian art, tombs, and mummies. For ancient Egyptians, scarabs symbolized rebirth and were good luck charms.

Studying mummies is not always simple. You cannot just find a mummy and look at it. Care must be taken to keep the mummy whole. It took the right conditions to preserve the mummy in the first place. The conditions must be kept up. If not, the mummy will not last. There may be nothing left to study.

Air is a big threat to mummies. Scientists once opened a mummy to study it. The mummy was coated in a substance like tar. When air touched the substance, it began to smolder, or burn slowly. Then, it flamed and turned the mummy to ash. Now we know that an exposed mummy does not last. Mummies must be studied without being exposed to air.

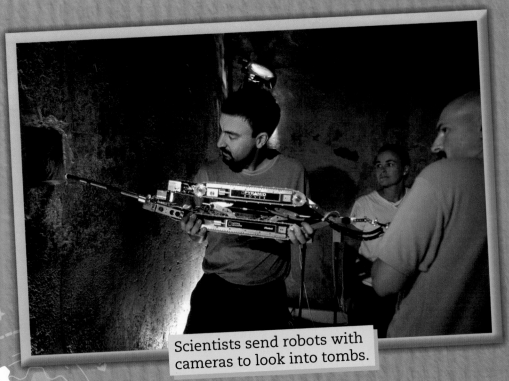

Scientists send robots with cameras to look into tombs.

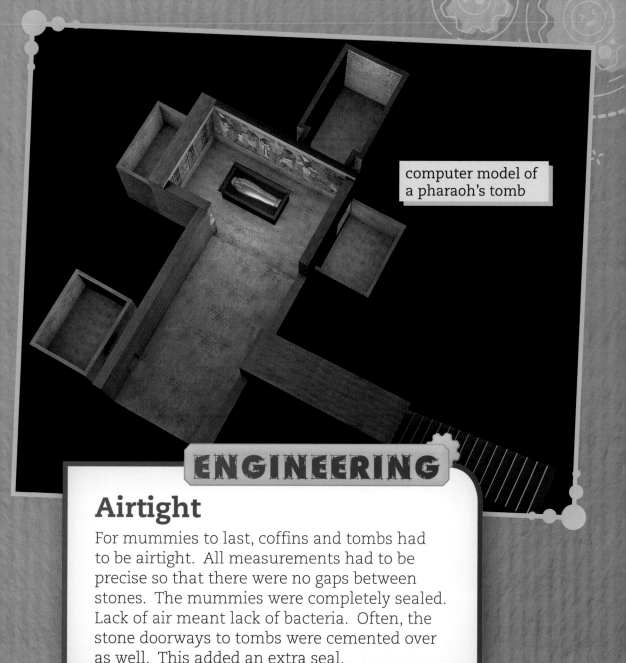

computer model of
a pharaoh's tomb

ENGINEERING

Airtight

For mummies to last, coffins and tombs had
to be airtight. All measurements had to be
precise so that there were no gaps between
stones. The mummies were completely sealed.
Lack of air meant lack of bacteria. Often, the
stone doorways to tombs were cemented over
as well. This added an extra seal.

Modern Tools

Mummies can be studied now in more depth than ever before. Tools exist to look inside them without cutting them open. Chemicals in the body and **DNA** can also be studied. They reveal a lot. They may show what the people ate, how they died, and more.

X-rays and computed tomography (CT) scans help scientists. They can look through coffins to see what is inside. Tiny cameras on long, thin tubes can also take a peek. This is done in the same way doctors look inside their patients without a scalpel. The mummies are kept whole. Better yet, they can be studied again as new tools are made.

Artists can also help. They use scans as models of the mummies. Then, they draw what the people may have looked like when they were alive.

mummy X-ray

Making the Past Present

CT scans are like X-rays. But CT scans are much more detailed than X-ray images. They show what is inside an object being scanned with incredible detail. Scientists scan mummies' bones and soft tissue. The scans can be stacked together using a computer program to create 3-D images. These scans can then be used to make models of the mummies using 3-D printers.

What Mummies Reveal

Modern tools can be used to give details about each mummy. They may tell the person's age at death and his or her overall health. They may tell how the person died.

The size and shape of a mummy's pelvic bone reveals whether it is male or female. A wider opening belongs to a female.

Arthritis on bones can show the person's age. Bones get rougher as people get older. Teeth show a child's age. Children lose and gain teeth at certain ages. The measurement of their long bones can also show a child's age. But poor nutrition can stunt growth.

Bones may also reveal the person's general health at death. Was the death sudden or due to illness? Can wounds be seen? Wounds may show how a person died.

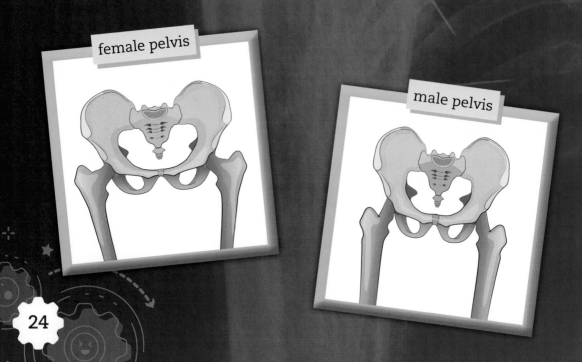

female pelvis

male pelvis

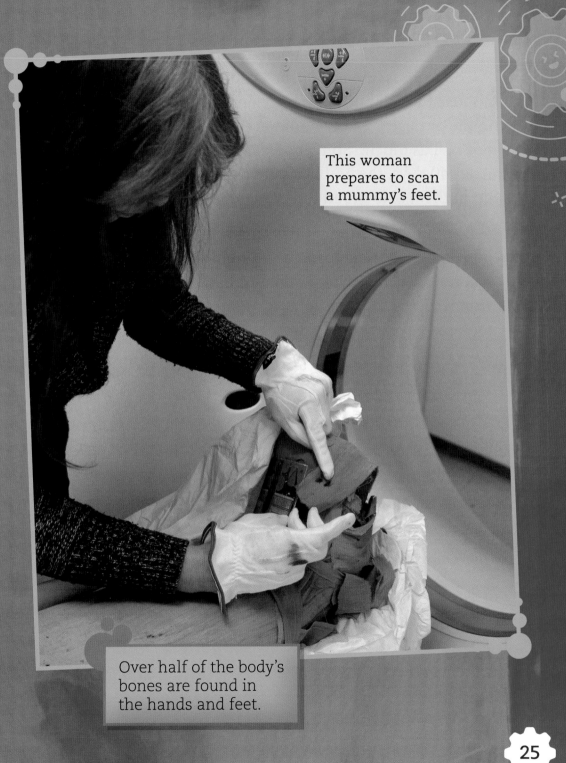

This woman prepares to scan a mummy's feet.

Over half of the body's bones are found in the hands and feet.

That's a Wrap

The truth is, the ideal process for making mummies was not used for all bodies. The people of Egypt were not equal in life or death. Many bodies were treated in ways that did not cost as much. Some bodies were just packed in natron. After 40 days, the body was given to the family. Burial was up to them. No grand tombs were in their future.

But simple methods still cost money. Even so, each person hoped to be made into a mummy. They wanted to be preserved. Everyone wanted a happy afterlife. It is no wonder Egyptians did so much to improve the process. It took many years. There was trial and error. But they stuck with it no matter what. They believed their lives depended on it.

mummified crocodile

mummified hawk
inside wooden coffin

Some animals were also made into
mummies. Sometimes, this was done
for religious reasons as offerings to
the gods. Other times, it was done so
the animal could go with the dead.

STEAM CHALLENGE

Define the Problem

A mummified cat has been found near the ancient city of Thebes. You have been hired to build a box to ship the mummy safely to a museum. Before the mummy is shipped, you must test your model to prove it will protect the mummy.

Constraints: Use no more than five materials, such as cardboard pieces, tape, glue, packing peanuts, straws, toothpicks, foam pieces, or scrap paper.

Criteria: Your model must protect a fragile item when dropped from a height of 1 meter (3 feet).

Research and Brainstorm

Why would a mummy need to be shipped in a special box? How will your box protect a mummy?

Design and Build

Sketch your design. What purpose will each part serve? What materials will work best? Build the model.

Test and Improve

Place a fragile item in your model. Drop it from 1 m (3 ft.) above the ground. Was the fragile item kept safe? Modify your design, and try again.

Reflect and Share

Was your design successful? How do you know?

Glossary

amulets—small objects worn to keep away bad luck

archaeologists—scientists who study remains (such as fossils, relics, artifacts, and monuments) of past human life and activities

artifacts—items made by humans that are of cultural or historical interest

assess—make a fact-based judgment

bogs—wet, spongy grounds that are usually found next to bodies of water, such as ponds

canopic jars—urns used to hold mummified organs and placed with their mummy in a tomb

desecrate—to damage or treat badly and without respect

dissected—surgically cut open and apart

DNA—the substance that contains genetic information in the cells of plants or animals

embalming—the process of treating a dead body so that it does not decay

innards—insides of a body

linen—natural fabric made from a plant called flax

natron—a salt-based powder found along the Nile that has the effect of killing bacteria

organisms—living things

preserved—to have been saved from decomposition

Index

Do you want to preserve the past?
Here are some tips to get you started.

"Develop a good work ethic by doing your homework and meeting deadlines. Read as much as you can about anatomy, forensics, anthropology, and ancient Egypt. I'm always amazed at how much you can learn about a person from analyzing a skeleton!" —**Dr. Douglas Ubelaker, Physical Anthropologist**

"It's important to know how to cause the least amount of damage for fragile objects like mummies so that they last for future study. In the museum, we use techniques to study the insides of mummies as well as the insides of coffins without ever having to open or disturb what is inside." —**Dr. David Hunt, Physical Anthropologist**